Kingdoms Within

Poetry from the Ashes Reborn

By Janine Palmer (Silver Moon) CHT
An Owl Feather Series

Other books by Janine Palmer

MAIN BOOKS: (First Series)

Divine Heretic – Standing Holy
Divine Heretic – In Christ Consciousness
Divine Heretic – Sacred Scribe
Divine Heretic – Mystical Fire
Divine Heretic – Alchemist
Divine Heretic – Hierophant
Divine Heretic – Hidden Keys
Divine Heretic – Wordsmith
Divine Heretic – Song of the Seraphim
Divine Heretic – Anima Mundi
Divine Heretic – Echo of Thunder
Divine Heretic – Sword of Truth
Divine Heretic – Flaming Sword
Divine Heretic – Compassionate Non-Conformist
Divine Heretic – Sacred Smoke Signals
Divine Heretic – Arrows of Light
Divine Heretic – The Edge of Inner Truth

JP SILVER MOON SERIES: (Second Series)

Magic Quill, Sacred Sword
Fire & Thunder of the Bard
Mystical Whispers of the Soul
Mystical Whispers of the Scribe

Quicksilver Ink
Owl Feather, Sacred Scribe
Recalling the Mystery, Goddess of Arc
On Winged Destrier
Points of the Queen's Crown
Whispers of the Woods
Soul Speak, Mystical Heart
Extracting Wisdom from Experience
By the Light of the Silver Moon
Divine Illumination
Spiritual Alchemy
Lady of Fire
On Ravens' Wings
Enchanted Perspectives
Shields & Swords of Light
From Mystic Realms
Winged Revelation
Mystical Whispers of the Heart
Mystical Whispers of Wisdom
Cloaked Mystery & Swords of Truth
Sacred Temple
Twinkling of Twilight
Swords & Shields of Light
From Mystic Realms
Shadow Dance
Glimpses of Soul
Journal Entries from the Dragon Path
The Midnight Moon

From the Angels of Avalon
Once a Knight
Through the Mists & Shadows
Ink of Angelic Fire
Sacred Dialogue
Bardic Fire
Smoke Signals from Sacred Fire
Arrow Flights
Forged in Sacred Flame
Through Mystical Grace
A Priestess and a Poet Scribe
Poetic Ripples
Beautiful Reflections in Tarnished Mirrors
A Gypsy, a Knight, and a Philosopher
Mystical Journeys & Sacred Travelers
Mystical Muse
Pirate Ships & Shakespeare's Lips
Little Voices Carried on the Wind
Love Notes to Self
Pirate Ships & Shakespeare's Lips
Mystical Keys of the Soul
Oak Leaves & Acorns
Grails of Silver & Gold
Foxes & Flowers
Poet's Treasures
Bard's Treasures
Poetry from the Ashes Reborn
Glimpses of Mystical Prayers

Poetic Pinpoints of Light
Mystical Keys of the Soul
Divine Messages & Sacred Seeds
From the Ashes of Heretic Fire
Notes from Sacred Realms
Thoughts Infused with Love
A Cottage in the Heart
The Castle of the Heart
Whispers from Sacred Realms
From Bardic Wisdom Keepers

OWL FEATHER SERIES: (Third Series)

Gatekeepers of Sacred Temples
Remembering Forgotten Worthiness
Reflections of Perceptions
Weaving Beauty with Gratitude
This Book
Poetic Ministrations
Treasure Boxes & Tea Parties
Reflections of Worthiness
Mystical Ink
Perspectives, Paradigms & Possibilities
Gypsy Moon Boom
Mystical Chit Chat

GENRE SPECIFIC BOOKS:
(Material Pulled from Main Books)

Energy Healing Wisdom
Spiritual Healing Wisdom
Divine Healing Wisdom
Rising Above Dogma
For Romance
Heart Speak
Romantic Reflections
Book of Worthiness
Apocalypse of Worthiness
Scriptures of Worthiness
Providence of Worthiness
Shamanic Energy Medicine
Sacred Shamanic Whispers
Shamanic Poetic Points of Light
Shamanic Healing Wisdom
Poetic Fire
Forged in Poetic Fire
Poetic Fire of the Soul

GENRE SPECIFIC BOOKS:
**(Material pulled from the JP Silver Moon Series
and Owl Feather Series)**

Sometimes, Always, Never
Sometimes, Then and Now

Souvenirs of the Soul
Bardic Passion Ignited
Poetic Flame Ignited
Forged in Poetic Flame
Pulse Point Poetry

Dedication

This book is dedicated to my family with deep love and to all the people who inspired me to write and to all poets and writers. The poetry contained herein is an acknowledgement to the healing powers of writing.

Writing about the importance of processing and releasing emotions becomes artistic expression. Energy needs to flow. These tales are about releasing those blocks. Trust the process of unfolding and spiritual evolvement.

Blessings, love, and light.

Janine Palmer (Silver Moon) CHT

Acknowledgment of Gratitude

I am grateful for the blessings along my path, even the ones disguised as piles of shite. We learn from everything and everyone.

I am thankful for friends and guides and for so many amazing things learned and for the energy healing modalities I've learned, including and especially shamanic training, which helped to remember things, ancient things, I had forgotten.

I am thankful of emotional and spiritual healing which is an ongoing process. I am thankful for the opportunity to be of service and to help others when and if I can, when and if they ask for it.

I am thankful for such beautiful wisdom regained. I'm thankful for the inspiration for the writing and for how I am guided, known, or unknown. I am thankful to be able to incorporate healing messages into the poems and messages.

I am thankful for what I've learned from spiritual teachers and biblical scholars and that I have always enjoyed reading which has opened me to so much knowledge and wisdom. I am grateful to all those who believed in me.

I want to say thank you to all the friends and family who have graciously supported me, taught me, and redirected me. So many blessings.

Janine Palmer (Silver Moon) CHT

Foreword

This little book reflects glimpses of experience and the wisdom gained from them. It reflects wounds, and the effects of the wounded who wound. It speaks of energy healing and forgiveness. It speaks of spiritual alchemy and the ascension of the spirit and the soul. It speaks of opening the door of the heart to love.

It speaks of battle scars and shedding skins and shells. It speaks of sacred temples and the fire of transformation. It speaks of rising above and moving beyond judgment, the spiraling, higher path to freedom through love and healing and releasing what does not serve. It speaks of the power of forgiveness. It speaks of things mystical and sacred. It speaks of magic.

It speaks of angels and dragons and divine love. It speaks of mirrors, treasures, keys and the mystical. It speaks of shadow and perspectives. It speaks of spirit, heart, soul, and light. It speaks of deeper truth beyond belief and hidden keys. It basically shares the depth of love revealed by life experiences.

Introduction

What is shared in my writings often comes from wisdom gained through experiences, sometimes very grueling experiences. What is shared is also tools and knowledge gained from many healing modalities and certifications as well as much study of religions, religious scholars, and spiritual teachers.

My work is for the purpose of reminding people to their worthiness and rising above judgement as far as condemnation of others due to lack of compassion or understanding.

These little stories offer information about healing self and stepping away from or letting go of toxic energies. Everyone interprets them differently. What I speak of comes from being shattered. Some of what I write comes from the parts of me which survived and endeavored to tell the tales and share what I learned.

Many of us do what we feel called to do for the collective, for the greater good…whatever our perception of that is. There are many unhealed wounds in this world, in people, in the earth, and in animals.
There are unhealed wounds in ancestral lines. These unattended wounds often cause people to go out and create more wounds.

We can do the work if we feel called to. The writing in this (and these) books are for those who have taken a step out on the path and are already moving out of stagnation and programming, or those who are ready to.

JP Silver Moon (CHT)

Contents

Sacred Temple

When transformation trumps tragedy,
And illusion is at rest,
When wisdom overrides ignorance,
We know we have been blessed.

Sacred Temple

Is darkness the draw?
Or the light underneath?
Is love still the highest?
Or the idol of belief?

Sacred Temple

Through behaviors destructive,
There are things we might learn,
Wisdom from experiences gathered,
And emotions that burn.

Sacred Temple

There might be truth in cruelty,
There might be truth in a lie,
Illusion like smoke obscuring clarity,
Greeting whispers as they fly.

Sacred Temple

Mother, sister, daughter,
Friend from a beautiful realm,
Soul deep and mysterious,
Drawing magic from her well.

Sacred Temple

In between the battles,
Real or perceived,
Is a field of balance,
Beyond all belief.

Sacred Temple

When happiness comes back into balance,
The weight may be released,
The door may remain boldly open,
In the absence of the thief.

Sacred Temple

Glimpses of Soul

Balanced

The king and his healer,
The king and his mage,
The queen and her parchment,
The tear on the page.

The mirth of the jester,
The kindness bestowed,
The forgiveness of trespasses,
The karma not owed.

Glimpses of Soul

Ribbons dance in a stormy breeze,
As we question what we believe,
Not clinging rigidly to egoic things,
But creating space for hearts to sing.

Glimpses of Soul

There are those we encounter along the pathways of life we call friends. We might call them teachers. They might be mirrors. We might embrace them, or we might reject them. They can teach us something about ourselves, even if we aren't aware of it.

Some people are friends of our friends or family and our souls simply recognize them. We might stay friends our entire lives and nothing might happen to disrupt that balance.

Other times people seem to just drift off in different directions or maybe they pull away from each other due to however life is directing them or things they don't want to talk about.

Sometimes we might annoy, irritate, or offend our friends due to our energy which we might not be aware of. We are all working through things others might not understand or might not be aware of.

We might offend them unknowingly. There are times we do or say something where no harm was intended, but people perceive themselves to be harmed and until its discussed, it can't be rectified.

We might accidentally poke an old wound. We might do something we think is helpful and supportive, but it might reopen something they'd rather keep closed.

So, cracks might form, and things might get wedged in the cracks. Things we might hold against someone and not discuss with them in order to facilitate healing and restore balance.

Sometimes we don't want the conflict. Sometimes maybe it seems easier to make someone the 'bad guy' as a reason to let go of something that has simply run its course.

There are so many things to be perceived through limited knowledge and so much that is harmed through misperception.

I am thankful for friends who have come and gone and for those who have stayed, even on the fringes as we all navigate different and similar pathways.

I am thankful for the teachers and healers who have graced my path and shared their gifts and wisdom with me.

I am sorry for the ones who have drifted away or if I drifted away. Sometimes when someone stops interacting with us, we might assume they just don't want to continue the friendship, but they might be going through something we aren't aware of.

Communication is such a powerful key to a door many of us prefer to keep open. There is love and attachment to those whom our soul recognizes, like a welcome embrace. Like a celebration of beauty.

This is simply a note of gratitude to all my beautiful teachers and a thank you for the closeness shared through the beauty of friendship.

Even when things happen that seem to tear us open and make us cry in sadness for what is lost through misperception and misunderstanding, there are fond memories of love through a type of honor which is timeless, and those pinpoints of light are never lost.

Glimpses of Soul

They were talking about friendships, and she told
her him friendships mean a lot to her.

He said, "I know and empathize with your
sensitivity to certain acquaintances and friendships.
And, how you're always on fresh new ground every
time you interact with them. That takes courage and
compassion."

Glimpses of Soul

When running the gauntlet,
Take time to admire,
Reflections of truth,
In Divinity's fire.

Glimpses of Soul

Mystical & Sacred

Something delicious sometimes calls,
A mystery or a memory still enthralls,
It might visit in dreams or through inspiration's gate,
Some call it destiny, some call it fate.

Mystical & Sacred

A basket of blessings,
Tools and gifts,
Shared with all beings,
Anchored or adrift.

Mystical & Sacred

Be not forgetful to entertain learning,
Remembering what you don't know,
Overlaying amnesia with awareness,
The recognition of your glow.

The light within glowing brighter,
The magic of your flame,
And how it adds to the collective,
Enhancing the blessings we all gain.

Janine Palmer (Silver Moon)

Mystical & Sacred

The kingdom of knowing,
The energy of grace,
The light beyond separation,
Lost or embraced.

Mystical & Sacred

Evolving Personal God(s)

What were you taught?
How were you trained?
Is it truth or illusion?
Or love unrestrained?

Are there facts still unknown?
Do you think the story is complete?
Is there separation and resistance?
Is there some need to compete?

Is perspective a ruler?
Is there room still to bend?
Are you aware of unfoldment?
From the colors which blend?

Are they flowing or stagnant?
The stories we tell?
Does what we proclaim to believe,
Come from a deep well?

Is there still treasure unburied?
Is there still truth to discover?
Have we fully learned to love?
All our sisters and brothers?

Amnesia that's fading,
As knowing comes in,
The evolving of consciousness,
Beyond all the din.

Beyond rigid belief systems,
Still incomplete,
Broader perspectives of God,
As love is replete.

Metanoia retranslated,
To go beyond the mind,
Back to divine truth,
Beyond space and time.

Realization of Source,
Beyond labels and groups,
Beyond hatred and fear,
To align with our truth.

Spirit Silver Moon

Mystical & Sacred

Exploring the rabbit hole,
And the treasure buried there,
Not everyone is interested,
In an otherworldly lair.

The tapestry tells a story,
However we might perceive,
Colorful timeless messages,
Which parts of us receive.

Mystical & Sacred

Sword, dagger or sewing needle,
Spinning wheel, yarn, and thread,
Moving beyond belief into knowing,
Acknowledging how we are blessed.

Mystical & Sacred

Finding the keys,
To my own subconscious locks,
As I process the feelings,
Of emotional blocks.

Mystical & Sacred

Divine Wisdom

She said, "You get busy and forget who you truly
are but others like me still see the beauty, kindness,
and empathy that you have on this world. I
appreciate you and I'm grateful for you."

Thank you, WB

Divine Wisdom

What we miss might still live in the heart,
Where no earthly illusion can tear it apart,
It lives in divinity and in our dreams.
In another realm, not as it seems.

Divine Wisdom

Gaining knowledge can be dangerous … to those
who gain something from your ignorance.

There are entities who would prefer people didn't
know how to heal themselves so they can profit
from the limited types of healing products and
procedures they might sell.

Those who want the power to decide what someone
can and cannot have access to due to the greed
which has veiled or suffocated love.

Study, learn and don't be afraid to make different
choices if they resonate with your soul and/or spirit.

Divine Wisdom

How I recognize, acknowledge, and honor the divine
in myself and others is my own learning experience.

When compassion guides me, I know I am on the
right path.

Divine Wisdom

There are people who are stuck in their
programming,
And you can't help them to disengage,
They must walk the path of discernment to discover,
When it's time to turn another page.

Some people take up the mighty pen,
And decide to write their own story's page,
Rather than following rigid interpretations,
Preceded by fear and rage.

So many different interpretations,
Which may or may not incite needless wars,
Some people unconsciously choose to remain stuck,
Behind ideology's darkened doors.

Janine Palmer (Silver Moon)

Divine Wisdom

God's Country

Studying the tapestries,
As life lessons and stories unfold,
To discover my inner truth,
Beyond what I've been taught or told.

God's country might be a pathway,
Leading me back to my light,
God's country might be a change in perspective,
Beyond perceptions of wrong and right.

God's country might be gathering knowledge,
And shedding ideologies untrue,
God's country might be infusing more love,
Into everything I do.

God's country might be in me,
There for me to discover,
God's country might be honoring the divinity,
In myself and every other.

God's country might be deep compassion,
For all beings upon this earth,
And the unfolding of it beautifully,
As part of our rebirth.

God, Goddess in its fullness,
Great spirit, Source of love,
The children remembering their divinity and
worthiness,
And the promptings of the dove.

The Triune unforgotten,
The Holy Spirit, the Paraclete,
Fullness not separated or fractured,
As love eloquently speaks.

Janine Palmer (Silver Moon)

Divine Wisdom

Energy Healing

He said, "You've done a lot of work on yourself. It's
so important how powerful it is to be able to change
perspective."

"Amen," she replied.

Energy Healing

She said the thunder went right through her,
What might it shake loose?
Would that it could dislodge the judgment,
That tightened ego's noose.

Energy Healing

There are people who are jealous of others and
rather than conquering or rising above the jealousy,
especially if they're not consciously aware of it, they
might cast the person aside so as not to feel irritated,
annoyed or triggered by them.

Energy Healing

There are those who won't hear you no matter how much you speak, shout or cry. Sometimes more is learned through silence and observation.

Some people would rather hold onto their beliefs than consider other perspectives or kernels of truth. They might even enjoy your suffering which might distract them from their own.

Most people feel entirely justified in so-called crimes or offenses they commit. We might not see our behaviors and actions as types of offenses. Maybe we are aware of our unkind behaviors and maybe we're not. Maybe we mean no harm at all.

Sometimes people will perceive wrongdoing and react to it, when what they perceived did not actually happen in the way they perceived it. Some people seem to want to have someone or something to hate and blame.

If it's directed at you, be present and honest with yourself and look within to why you do what you do. Is it fair and balanced in however it affects people around you? People whose stories you don't know in their fullness.

Energy Healing

There are parts of our wounds or scars which might
still have something to say even after we think we
have healed, and we will recognize it by the emotion
in our voices when we talk about it.

Energy Healing

Gateways

What is interpretation?
And how is it applied?
Would we recognize conditioning?
Or interwoven lies?

Do we react to the external?
Is our inner compass intact?
Do we glow more brightly?
When we take our power back?

Who are the storytellers?
And what do they perceive?
How much truth is passed down or hidden?
Through what we may or may not believe?

Fundamentalism and literalism,
Might be stumbling blocks,
We might find that we are challenged,
To find keys to many locks.

Researching bits of wisdom,
To determine what resonates,
On a journey to recognize and remember,
The light shining on new gates.

Energy Healing

She might have come so far out the other side of the
rabbit hole that you might not recognize her.

It might be an escape from the prison of false
ideologies through the process of recognizing truth
and stepping back into her own power.

Giving power away to external forces of
manipulation is something some people outgrow or
rise above. The path of ascension.

Energy Healing

Fire of Transformation

Embers & Memories

A burning stake,
Once upon a time,
A calling created,
To heal a crime.

A crown or a sword,
Armor or cape,
And the knowledge and wisdom,
That ignorance can't take.

Fire of Transformation

The loss might make the heart sigh,
Love and wisdom fill in the gaps,
Forgiveness lifts you higher,
As you animate your map.

Fire of Transformation

The ink is quicksilver,
Of emotion that flows,
The feelings so tender,
The blush of the rose.

Fire of Transformation

Does any part of us feed off drama?
Or any judgment we create or perceive?
Are we an unknowing prisoner?
Of what we think we believe?

Fire of Transformation

It might be like an escape, disengaging or
disentangling oneself from manipulative control
systems designed to look like a comfort zone or a
rescue effort one must subscribe to.

That which people defend through ego and fight for
in the absence of fuller knowledge, unknowingly
giving their power away.

People conditioned to believe they're unworthy and
must be rescued by anything other than their own
awareness and recognition of their own divinity.

Fire of Transformation

Principles of Translation

It said that things are lost in translation,
It's known that much can be misunderstood,
Different experiences create different beliefs,
The views from where we've stood.

Different perceptions and perspectives,
Different ways we see,
Different ways we hear, feel, and react,
Different ways we're bound or free.

Translations of cultures and stories,
Information missing, known or not,
The divinity in and around us,
So many of us forgot.

When it's love that speaks the loudest,
When compassion leads the way,
There are always many different ways,
That we may seize the day.

Janine Palmer (Silver Moon)

Fire of Transformation

Ancient Ancestral Narratives

That which is taught and passed down,
From different cultures and perspectives believed,
May or may not contain full truth,
What realization is or isn't achieved?

How do we learn if we don't study?
How do we ascend out of amnesia's lair?
How do we maintain balance through compassion?
What is and isn't fair?

Ancestral narratives passed down,
From what information was at hand,
But what about knowledge that was hidden?
In the free will zone of man.

How beautiful are our pathways,
What do we leave behind?
What do we take with us?
Is it cruel or is it kind?

Janine Palmer (Silver Moon)

Fire of Transformation

Spiritual Alchemy

Some people stand on slippery decks in storms
pulling up the anchors that kept their ancestors stuck
in turbulent seas.

Spiritual Alchemy

He said, "Do you have any wishes?"

She answered, "That's a good question. I am
thankful for what I have and the ability to create.
There are things the heart desires if desire is the
right word.

There might be the wish to give and receive love at
higher levels than humans seem to be capable of. To
experience a depth of connection that makes the
heart and soul sing."

Spiritual Alchemy

Music and steeples and those they might touch,
And what's in between, which ignorance might
crush,
Of gross misperception we must beware,
As lack of knowledge can rip and tear.

Spiritual Alchemy

A lonely place, a void to fill,
Memories are stories, vibrant still,
As chapters are written, in dark or light ink,
Love is the elixir all of us drink.

Spiritual Alchemy

Avenues & Pathways

Away they go or away you go,
Realizing there's always more to know.

Down a different path, so much to learn,
Gifts to give away and those which burn.

A trail of emotion, fairy dust or flame,
A learning experience or cruelest game.

Is it stuck or does it flow,
Is the scar invisible or does it glow?

Spiritual Alchemy

Meeting what becomes familiar,
Experiences painful sometimes,
Due in part to misunderstanding,
And truth we can't yet find.

Redirection to other paths,
New friends along the way,
Some are our greatest teachers,
Whether or not they choose to stay.

Spiritual Alchemy

It might behoove us to continue to gather more information to better understand the people and the world around us. False judgement and unnecessary resentment are poisonous to our being.

Spiritual Alchemy

Worthiness & Wings

I might not remember parts that are true,
But souls I remember like the beauty of you,
Many experiences, related or not,
The wisdom I've gained, even when I forgot.

Worthiness & Wings

Is it some kind of evil, or is it just fear?
What comes from amnesia, remaining unclear,
Is it old wounds or loss of faith?
Until love is restored, through truth always great.

Beyond false belief, a limiting stage,
Past misunderstandings and dissonant rage,
Letting go of illusion, a terrible snare,
To return to the love, which exists everywhere.

Worthiness & Wings

Buildings of mystery, built long before,
Before belief systems were tainted, through
imbalanced doors,
Where ego's not Master and love is still King,
In full sacred balance, enhanced by its Queen.

Worthiness & Wings

In balance are aspects, not at war with each other,
With nothing to prove, whether sister or brother,
Love, the experience, a brilliant gate,
Back to our wholeness, not tethered by hate.

Worthiness & Wings

There might be instances where you open up to
someone about something traumatic you
experienced, and they will try to invalidate it and the
emotions which are still healing. The roads we walk
might be lonely for a reason.

Worthiness & Wings

It might be true that we should not allow ourselves
to be victims, but that doesn't mean people won't try
to victimize us.

Worthiness & Wings

There are events which strengthen us,
even if it feels like they tear us apart first.

Worthiness & Wings

Blessed Be Our Magic

A pendulum swinging back and forth,
Adjustments made on every course,
Forgiveness like a crown, of holy thorns,
The ways in which the spirit is reborn.

Detaching from programs,
Expectations no more,
When love replaces fear,
It reveals sacred doors.

Blessed Be Our Magic

He said, "There is something
magical about your home,"

Blessed Be Our Magic

Resonance Combined

How my heart opened,
And smiled for a time,
That spectacular moment,
When resonances combine.

When language is like medicine,
That nurtures the soul,
When my countenance shimmered,
With an effervescent glow.

When an experience seemed wonderful,
And my heart felt great joy,
Like a gift preordained,
Which destiny deploys.

Blessed Be Our Magic

He said, "When I am overwhelmed, I'm driven by other thoughts that I want to sweep from my mind. I have good and bad sides but in the end my good side always wins and I am aware of having made mistakes.

A darkness dwells in me and I try to send it away. Sometimes that darkness helps me a lot in my work, in what I do, because I have no fears. But sometimes it makes me uncomfortable with others.

If I cast out that darkness what would become of me? A fearful man? A man without words? Maybe I have to live with it but know how to dose it."

She said, "In meditation ask why the darkness is there. Ask it. Speak to it. Sometimes it might be something connected to our wounded inner child."

He said, "Yes!! It's precisely this wounded past of mine that keeps me going, as if it were a stimulus for life. I love talking to you. I love your way of answering. I love your doctrine of life."

Blessed Be Our Magic

He said, "With you I can speak openly, like an open book. With you I am myself because I feel in my heart that you are a beautiful soul. Thank you for your friendship."

Blessed Be Our Magic

He said, "You put yourself out there sometimes my
dear and sometimes those slings and arrows come
back and it's not fair because I know your motives
are good.

You have the courage of your conviction to search
out truth and have found and overcome those slings
and arrows. You're strong and capable of
weathering any storm. I quite admire that."

Blessed Be Our Magic

He said, "Self-examination shows awareness. The
sadness is a temporary side effect of moving on up.
The spiritual life has thorny reminders."

She said, "Sometimes we must drop the rose or
leave it behind because the thorns are too destructive
and painful. Sometimes it's best to admire it in its
natural state and not try to bring it with us."

Blessed Be Our Magic

Deeper Truth

Many so-called religions are highly programmed, conditioned and/or brainwashed. Some people move beyond belief and into knowing, into the kingdom within, recognizing that God is within themselves and others.

Not something separate from themselves. Certain belief systems are very limited and rigid in their viewpoints or perceptions and keep people stuck in a type of dogmatic box. They don't seem open to allow people to move beyond fear-based beliefs which are designed to make them conform.

Some people step into their divinity and move away from that which would keep them shackled. We all have that choice, but first we must recognize it.

Deeper Truth

When people are firmly entrenched in believing
something you know is untrue, there is probably
nothing you can do or say to show them or teach
them what they are unaware of until they are ready
to step out of that stagnation or prison.

There is so much truth unseen and unrecognized all
around us and within us. People react to what they
believe, creating suffering through rigidness,
possibly blaming someone for an imagined or
perceived offense. Falsehood animated through
distortion and reacted to through wounds or
emotions.

You might choose to step away from another's
negative energy to exist in a more peaceful place and
they might feel offended or powerful. They might
think their provoking behavior is proving a point
when it might only be keeping them stuck in a type
of hell which they create which you don't have to
participate in.

Deeper Truth

Poisoners

The destruction through the ages,
Fueled by false belief,
That people tout(ed) as holy,
But it's really an undiscovered thief.

Beliefs rooted too long in fear,
And what they might create,
How they harm the innocent,
Through obscure, nefarious gates.

At the time of the inquisition,
'Poisoners' was translated to 'witches',
Groupthink and fear spread like hellfire,
Burning the patriarchy's imbalanced britches.

We who must experience,
Whatever we create,
The diabolical road of realization,
And what comes from fear and hate.

Prisoners of belief systems,
As yet though, still unknown,
Until love becomes stronger than fear and ego,
And the light of truth is shown.

Janine Palmer (Silver Moon)

False Shadows

Miss Interpretation tripping,
Miss Understanding fell,
Miss Perception suffering,
Through avenues of hell.

Reinstating sovereignty,
Disentangling from false beliefs,
Only when we begin to see the fallacy of separation,
From God or you and me.

When our spark of light becomes brighter,
As truth now enters in,
As the veil continues to be lifted,
Exposing false shadows of sin.

Integrity trumps self-righteousness,
Humbleness in flow,
As we open to remember,
The love we always know.

Janine Palmer (Silver Moon)

Deeper Truth

Historical stories defended,
Truth that was taken away,
Teachings that were hidden,
And the consequence of decay.

The loss of certain knowledge,
Stolen, obscured, or attacked,
As we walk through darkened shadows,
Misdirected then and now through lack.

Deeper Truth

A crown of twigs,
Suits her well,
An angel's voice,
A ringing bell.

A vessel of beauty,
Pure and true,
Navigating amnesia,
Weaving love through.

Deeper Truth

The gifts passed down from our ancestors
are treasures to be discovered in ourselves.

Deeper Truth

Mirror, Mirror

There are a lot of people who have different
perceptions of religions and what they are or are not.
They might talk of their viewpoint on something that
stems from their experiences or what they were
taught. They are simply speaking of what they know
or think they know at this time.

What I mean by that is that belief isn't the same as
knowing. Some people don't venture far beyond
what they adopt(ed) as belief. Others become
seekers and most likely discover that there is much
more to what they thought was 'true'. More to the
fullness of what and who we are that cannot be
limited by any manmade religion.

Mirror, Mirror

He said, "Tell me, what's more beautiful in this world without love? Art, poetry, sculpture, music, does not originate without love. Open your heart and reflect."

Mirror, Mirror

Spires and points and pyramids that reach,
For the energy forgotten and what
prophets might teach,
Sacred geometry unfolding, as frequencies sing,
The blessings we are and the blessings we glean.

Mirror, Mirror

Sometimes people will say something that isn't true on some level, but on another level, it contains truth. Sifting through it might be the tricky part.

Mirror, Mirror

Some people grow up 'religious' in certain ways adhering to what they were taught was 'right'. But maybe there are aspects of that which aren't fully understood. There is more to be known and that information might come from different sources. The heart and soul will recognize what resonates. That which comes from a vibration beyond fear.

Many religions are fear-based in that they use fear to control people, passed down for generations. They function from interpretations or misinterpretations of scriptures. If people don't 'seek' they might not find or discover that there is more to know than what they were taught to believe. Some people might observe or experience people of certain denominations of certain religions or cults behaving in ways contrary to what they proclaim to follow and believe.

Such as not treating their brethren in kind, gracious and loving ways. They are coming from a judgmental self-superiority and the belief that only their church is absolutely correct, which of course might be coming from the ego. Some people memorize scripture and then use it as weaponry against others they deem or perceive to be in error. A vicious cycle of stagnation, possibly destructive.

But there are further scriptures of the teachings of Jesus many people haven't investigated. Perhaps it isn't allowed as if they don't actually have free agency. Some people don't want their illusions shattered by deeper truths.

There are those who become 'seekers' as Jesus recommended and they find something completely different than what they thought they believed, and it can be so refreshing and liberating. But it might entail stepping out of dogmatic boxes, rigid programming and what we discoverer to be false indoctrination.

Jesus was arguing with the priests in the temple at age 12. There is much about Jesus that isn't told in the Bible which we can still learn if we're not afraid of discovery and that our perspectives might change. He advised against certain things the churches were doing and adhering to.

There are many people on this planet through the millennia who discover a calling, and they speak a truth that might be different from what others believe and they might be attacked for it. Just because someone shares knowledge from a different experience and endeavors to remind people of their worthiness, doesn't make them a wolf in sheep's clothing.

"Let brotherly love continue. Be not forgetful to entertain strangers: for thereby some have entertained angels unawares. Remember them that are in bonds, as bound with them; and them which suffer adversity, as being yourselves also in the body." Hebrews 13: 2-9.

And then there is the breaking of bonds.

It might just be that they are on a mission from or for God in a way some people don't recognize. There are, however, many people who do recognize the messages about the spark of the love of God. For far too long and for too many generations people have been ingrained to feel unworthy and that is a nefarious kind of darkness.

We all have a spark of the divine. But it is said that mankind has made God in its image. What light shines beyond the realm of the ego? The ego which is so protective and needs to strengthen sense of self? The Christ Consciousness might be about recognition of worthiness and rising out of or ascending out of the dogma and the indoctrination. To realign with love. Some people are very aware that we have a spark of God in us, a spark of the divine. That beauty of love which glows from within and radiates out to different degrees. How do we learn to acknowledge and share that gift?

There are many types of messengers. It's up to the person to determine whether it has any meaning to them. Some people might not be ready to hear it.

They might not be ready to step out of the programming that might feel like a type of comfort zone. There are areas in our lives which might be stagnant where we aren't learning or remembering from whence, we came.

When people truly study from knowledgeable sources and from more direct interpretations from the ancient languages, that light begins to glow brighter. Scriptures translated from Hebrew or Greek or Aramaic to Latin and then to English lose something in the translation.

Thcy are replaced with similar words, but not the same words and so there is or might be a different and false understanding which gets forged into a belief which may not be wholly accurate. When we believe things that aren't true, we might suffer. Things happen in our lives to crack us out of our shells so to speak. That which shifts us, that which rocks what we thought was our foundation because there is something we are supposed to discover.

People will find fault and judge. They might
condemn someone unfairly. Imbalance. Lacking
information. Maybe they are correct and maybe they
are incorrect and don't know it. What comes through
ego and what comes through grace? Can we tell the
difference?

The pathway of rediscovering love and allowing it to
shine is a shadowy path through forbidden forests
and the fog of illusion.

When people go within, to the kingdom within, they
might find more truth than they do from systems
outside of themselves which they try diligently to
adhere to. Does it come from love or fear?

Mirror, Mirror

Battle Scars & Shedding Skins

There are those who attack others to defend their programming or beliefs which they don't realize isn't the fullness of truth.

What you know to be truth, that which the ego doesn't need to try to defend, is a deep knowing that can't be taken from you and doesn't need to be defended.

Battle Scars & Shedding Skins

There are religions that use 'sin' or the misunderstanding of what it supposedly means as a weapon to keep people in fear, to control them and make them feel unworthy.

The correct translation of 'to sin' means to miss the point or to miss the mark. It's an archery term. There is much to learn and much to unlearn.

Battle Scars & Shedding Skins

Profiteering

Profiting from outrage,
Fearmongering like a disease,
Extremism out of balance,
As chaotic as you please.

What comes to fill the vacancies?
Where we seem disconnected from Source,
What creeps into those hollow spaces?
Of resentment, regret, and remorse?

If we fill the void with the highest love,
We will begin to notice a shift,
If we let go of burdens we're carrying,
We make room for waiting gifts.

Too many people seem to be,
Influenced by energy that is 'dark',
Not recognizing their own power,
Not kindling their own spark.

Too many trends and fads,
Leading us down shadowy paths,
Until we come into our own knowing,
And remember how to laugh.

Outside sources don't have power over us,
Unless we give that power away,
Pull that grungy curtain back,
And tell the little man you will not play.

Confusion like a toxic fog,
Swirling all around,
Until it gets stuck in the holes of wounds,
And common sense can't quite be found.

Peer pressure by some shady design,
Trying to reel us in,
Until we can hear the voice of something higher,
Whispering beyond the din.

That voice of our truer self,
Which doesn't answer to dark lords,
But smiles in divine light,
As we continue to cut cords.

No more profiteering from ignorance,
When our divinity is recognized,
As we step back into our collective light,
Beyond amnesia and false disguise.

Janine Palmer (Silver Moon)

Battle Scars & Shedding Skins

Wings of terror or angelic delight,
To awaken the heart and the soul's dark night,
The crumbling of belief systems, the eradication of
greed,
And the healing through love, where the cracks
made us bleed.

Battle Scars & Shedding Skins

Some might say she's too sensitive, others might say
she's too closed off, too direct or maybe too
mystical.

She knows what misunderstanding creates and that
friendships are fragile. She's still learning to let go
and fill the cracks with love.

Battle Scars & Shedding Skins

There are those who do you dirty in that they are
underhanded and conniving in what they take or
attempt to take from you.

It's interesting when you look back on it later and
realize they did you a favor because it redirected you
away from where you didn't need to be.

It rerouted you from what would have been a rocky,
treacherous road but you couldn't see it at the time.
So, relief and gratitude overlay the illusion of
heartbreak.

Perspective is powerful.

Battle Scars & Shedding Skins

Treasure & Keys

When darkness drips onto the page,
It might transform one's pain or rage,
When truth escapes and deigns to speak,
Flowing emotion, no longer a thief.

When tears unshed, turn to ink,
When new perspectives change the way we think,
On the path to taking our power back,
Where gains come forth from what was lack.

Treasure & Keys

Down some road, a beautiful path,
Where heartache overlaid what made us laugh,
Where mirrors were tarnished by
experiences of flame,
And signposts were burned not to return again.

Treasure & Keys

Vacancies of knowledge,
Thrones hijacked by thieves,
Valleys of sacred healing,
To heal the bereaved.

Memories from past battles,
And the lessons not yet learned,
As we pull from the smoking ashes,
What ignorance hasn't burned.

Treasure & Keys

The art of communication,
Differs hither and yon,
It probably depends upon,
What type of path you're on.

Some friendships might be deeper,
For reasons still unknown,
Or it may have been duly acknowledged,
That a soul connection has been shown.

That feeling that you know someone,
Even a person you haven't met,
And through dialogue you can be yourself,
With integrity and respect.

To be able to be fully open,
About philosophical and esoteric things,
Can sometimes be refreshing,
When the soul can really sing.

An avenue of learning,
Not a shallow or physical thing,
Just a friend the soul remembers,
And the gift that knowing brings.

When it's not a competition,
But a recognition of something more,
When we find we're absolutely brave enough,
To open our heart's door.

A mystical, magical encounter,
To learn more about ourselves,
Through the magic of communication,
And where we choose to dwell.

Not expecting any outcome,
From the celebration of friends,
Just walking a similar path,
And flowing when it bends.

Janine Palmer (Silver Moon)

Treasure & Keys

Being vindictive is like kicking the rungs off the ladder out of hell. To take your power back from hatred is a courageous endeavor requiring a depth of honesty with self.

Treasure & Keys

Vibrance

On the side of the road,
Vibrant flowers of blue,
Inspiring memories,
Of the beauty of you.

The light in the heart,
How you speak to the soul,
Reminding others of love,
That had forgotten to flow.

The magic of knowing,
Recognizing what's real,
And the courage to feel it,
The emotion we feel.

Janine Palmer (Silver Moon)

Treasure & Keys

Suffering & Shadow

Beware of what is meant to confuse and enrage.
That which is stealthily meant to hijack one's energy
through reaction to stupidity. That which targets
wounds and weaknesses and manipulates through
fear.

Suffering & Shadow

He said, "Don't let yourself be influenced by people.
Arise. You have a 7th light that others cannot see.
You don't have to explain to anyone. Your life is
different from ignorant people.

Never forget we are the light. Life is this. There are
no explanations. Go further. Everything is messed
up in the world."

How can we create change from within ourselves?

Suffering & Shadow

Cold Shoulder Faith

She's the queen of the cold shoulder,
She thinks religion told her so,
To be cold and so superior,
To those she deems 'below'.

So unlike the Lord she praises,
Not knowing how to heal,
And by her self-justified actions,
She knows not what she steals.

Suffering & Shadow

Actions often create reactions. We respond or react
to things, or we don't. Whatever we do or don't do
reveals much about us. We act or react due to what
and how we feel and what it might trigger.

We might react to something that isn't what it
seems, and not know it. That which takes our
energy. We might struggle or suffer due to our
thoughts about misinformation.

Suffering & Shadow

He tried to be savior for someone else,
Without enough healing for himself,
Missing soul fragments and those who're drawn in,
Might become victims, of games we can't win.

Beware of disrespect and disregard,
Wolves in sheep's clothing are real,
The pitfalls of linear thinking and limited
perspectives,
Trampling emotions, illusionary love affairs steal.

Suffering & Shadow

Fire Speaks

What are the stories,
Of the fire I breathe?
What experiences forgotten,
To which wisdom cleaves?

What is learned through experiments?
And how is it used?
How do we comfort?
How do we soothe?

How does my healing,
Differ from yours?
What treasure or debris,
Washes up on our shores?

What comes from our knowing,
Whether truth or belief,
Who is in charge,
The preacher or thief?

When do we become the master,
Of our very own path?
When love is most powerful,
And truth is our staff.

Not the rigid beliefs,
Of separation's snare,
But the truth of divinity,
Which exists everywhere.

Janine Palmer (Silver Moon)

Suffering & Shadow

Whispers from the Heart

He said, "I would love to touch your hair and feel your fragrance. What should I say other than I love every little thing about you."

Whispers from the Heart

She said, "There are things that we sense and feel
and know and perhaps things that we don't know.
Also, there is much we don't know we don't know."

Whispers from the Heart

Familiar Grin

Drawn by horses, two not four,
A gothic coach stopped near her door,
A man of knowing, a familiar grin,
He extended a hand and invited her in.

A twilight sky in Autumn woods,
Gloves and hats or cloaks with hoods,
A mysterious journey in changing light,
To experience the feeling of nature's delight.

Her fascination intrigued his senses,
Her smile melted any lingering defenses,
The clip clop of hooves, over the forest path,
And the delightful chuckle, of his hearty laugh.

Whispers of the Heart

He said, "I love your soul too much. Your sensitivity, your way of being and many other things. I shouldn't say that, but I can't lie. I like you terribly in all your ways. Forgive me if I'm blunt."

She said, "Thank you. That's nice of you to say. You show me aspects of myself I otherwise might not see."

He said, "We are both polite and our knowledge is clean and clear with a lot of respect for each other. Let me say this, I adore you in all your phases."

She said, "I appreciate your method of communication, your directness, honesty, and bravery. Your ability to communicate and what you say speaks to me on a soul level, even though we speak different languages and it's done through translation.

You don't really know me, but you feel your soul knows me. I think people forget who they are, including me. It's nice to be reminded."

Whispers from the Heart

Certain languages ring a bell,
Which might draw us in like a mystical spell,
How much is truth, we must dig deep,
To sift for the treasure, we're meant to keep.

Whispers from the Heart

He said, "I stay on social media
to read what you write."

Whispers from the Heart

She is poetry he turns into song.

Whispers from the Heart

Light through the Cracks

A breath of memory,
To spark the heart,
The treasures plucked,
From shadows dark.

The truth of love,
The brightest force,
No need for fear,
No false remorse.

Light through the Cracks

Forests dark within the heart,
The flame inside the brightest spark,
A love so gentle still untold,
An energy fierce and wise and bold.

Light through the Cracks

Freak Show

Welcome to the circus,
And all the media hype,
In a land where people use the law for immoral
things,
Dark fruit overripe.

There are criminals who slither between the lines,
And people who are attacked for truth and strength,
The wool pulled over our eyes,
Be careful what you drink.

Right and wrong now twisted,
Into the opposite of what they are,
Enemy camps and lies sold as truth,
The door to hell ajar.

Manipulation and corruption,
Agendas from brimstone's lair,
Where certain beings have no concept,
Of what it means to play fair.

Fear mongering is big business,
In sectors far and wide,
Those who profit from outrage,
As weasels sneak and hide.

The depth of what we each might feel,
May or may not be entirely real,
Misperception is a fickle host,
And which reactions hurt the most?

Light through the Cracks

He said, "I'm an open book. I have no secrets. I
express what I feel. I have a lot of flaws but I'm
loyal and I don't lie."

She said, "I'm the same. I'm very direct and prefer
to be open about things but some people aren't ready
for it or can't handle it. I'm loyal too, but I've also
learned to be loyal to myself and that's something
not everyone might understand.

Maybe when we're afraid to make certain changes
we're living a lie, so to speak, by not knowing how
to pursue what might be better for our soul. As you
said before, lacking confidence.

When we've been through something traumatic, we
might hesitate before entering into a similar situation
again. So, we make the best of what we have. Is it
right or wrong? That depends on many things,
especially perspectives."

Light through the Cracks

Haunted or Holy

The fire in the hearth tells stories,
Which the heart may or may not want to hear,
And memories might be liars,
In the absence of our tears.

Truth is recognized by the soul,
The compass, the sacred guide,
On a journey to remember,
The beauty we cannot hide.

We might be haunted, but we are holy,
The challenges which cause us to know ourselves,
What we consciously or unconsciously create,
Is it heaven or is it hell?

Do we take responsibility for our actions?
Or would we rather find fault and blame?
Is there ice around our hearts?
Or do we fan the flame?

We might be haunted by the mystery,
And that which we don't yet see,
We might be shackled by rigid perspectives,
Until we move from I to we.

Feeling justified in thoughts and actions,
Which might be harmful to another,
Too disconnected from Source,
For happiness to be recovered.

Until we remember that we are holy,
When the depth of the heart finally speaks,
An open heart is mighty,
Unsusceptible to dark thieves.

The holy from which we were created,
The holy which we forgot,
When we descended to this earth plane for learning,
To discover what we are and what we are not.

To remember to love one another,
To discover how to heal,
To learn the power of spiritual discernment,
Of what is an isn't real.

To step out of rigid belief systems,
Which shackle us to a cave,
To rise out of the falsest fear,
To overcome the knave.

Janine Palmer (Silver Moon)

Spoken from the Soul

She realized that self-doubt is a shield to an inner
mirror connected to the highest love and she can't
love anyone beyond the barrier of their wounds or
her own.

Spoken from the Soul

They were having a dialogue about her taking a break from social media. She wanted a rest.

She said, "Who cares if I take a break from social media?"

He said, "It matters to me if you take a break, because without you it would be nothing and sad without you."

She said, "That's kind of you to say but that's why I leave messenger open. As we know there are a lot of dark forces out there trying to interfere with lighter things."

He said, "The dark forces can never get in the way with your flash of light. Yes, you have messenger open, but it's nice to read your poems on social media. You have to manifest your inner light."

She said, "I wrote several short poems today. I'll post them tomorrow. Today is for rest."

He said, "Get your butt back on there and manifest your glow. I love your mystery and your light and other aspects about you."

She said, "I don't know why I'm mysterious to some people. Someone else also said that about me."

He said, "Let me tell you this, you have a special
charm."

Spoken from the Soul

She said, "Sometimes I observe things I'm sensitive
to. I try to handle myself with calm, balanced
fairness, kindness, and grace as much as possible.
But sometimes people bring out the dragon flame in
me."

Spoken from the Soul

Branches

What relationships do you nurture?
What relationships do you mend?
What relationships do you throw away,
Because you know not how to bend?

How susceptible are you to jealousy?
And how it can become a terrible thief?
How successful are you at making peace?
And transmutation of your grief?

How often do you blame someone?
For something that's untrue?
Are you misled by certain beliefs,
You don't realize mislead you?

What aspects are in need of healing?
What trauma still holds sway?
What whispers from your heart and soul?
What 'sin' does wisdom overlay?

What have you learned from experience,
That changed your perspective as you learned?
What dead branches from the tree,
Need now to be burned?

Spoken from the Soul

He said, "Do you think with everything I have to do I would look for you? I do it because my soul feels good with you. I'm not a man who gives compliments to women, but with you I feel something different. I'm not afraid to say that my soul loves you. I just feel good with you. I'm myself."

Spoken from the Soul

Crumbling Walls

She discovered a block,
Between what she feels, and she speaks,
She was fortunate when,
She let go of belief.

When she stepped into knowing,
When she learned new ways to love,
When she listened to the promptings,
Of the Holy Spirit, the dove.

When the rigidness became painful,
Too tight and too stiff,
She had to learn to let go,
Of the pain of the rift.

To not hold too tightly,
To things loved and lost,
To honor herself,
No matter the cost.

Janine Palmer (Silver Moon)

Spoken from the Soul

Beyond Belief

Instead of billboards that say, 'Jesus Saves Sinners', which is manipulating people through their unnecessary guilt programs…what if it said, "Jesus Restores Love', which we've lost, which might be perceived as sin.

The correct translation of 'to sin' means to miss the point or miss the mark. Not the twisted heinous connotation of unworthiness certain churches and religions have made it out to be, which is false.

That which has been used to control the masses until people begin to wake from the dream and step boldly out of the shadows of dogmatic boxes.

Beyond Belief

People can try to shove their beliefs and preferences
down other people's throats,
but those people might barf it up because
it's distasteful, foul, or poisonous to them somehow.

Beyond Belief

Shedding the cult,
Labeled as belief,
Distraction from truth,
No longer a thief.

Back to sovereign love,
So many prophets have taught,
Not egoic ideologies,
Too many people have bought.

Beyond Belief

How about no to digital prisons,
No to slave systems far and wide,
And yes, to love in the highest,
Where darkness cannot hide.

Beyond Belief

Moonlit Crown

The brightest jewel,
In her homespun crown,
Is compassionate light,
To pass around.

A quiet place,
A reflecting pond,
Where words have wings,
To soar upon.

Dancing flames,
An eagle's stare,
Treasure hidden,
A dragon's lair.

A faery realm,
And Avalon,
Where moonlight shimmers,
And truth responds.

Janine Palmer (Silver Moon)

Beyond Belief

He said, "Poems have wolves inside."

She said, "Wolves? Mine have dragons."

Beyond Belief

He said, "I feel like a false warrior with the soul of a
clown who in the best moments can ruin everything.
People don't know me. I may look like a warrior,
but inside I'm fragile like a child, very sensitive."

She said, "Not a false warrior. A heyoka, maybe.
Very empathic. We are all sensitive and try to hide it
from the world."

Beyond Belief

Sacred Clown

The heyoka is a kind of sacred clown in the culture of the
Sioux (Lakota and Dakota people) of the Great Plains of
North America. The heyoka is contrarian, and satirist,
who speaks, moves, and reacts in an opposite fashion to
the people around them.

Above definition from Google/Wikipedia

148

Metaphoric Light

She's gentle and compassionate,
She's feral and fierce,
She's a balm for the wound,
And the sword that might pierce.

Metaphoric Light

Ripples

Cast aside,
Or so it seemed,
Ripples in the water,
Or was it the dream?

Unbound from illusion,
Through the rabbit hole,
Somewhere in the darkness,
I discovered my glow.

Metaphoric Light

He said, "May I remind you,
your Grace, you have a dragon."

Metaphoric Light

He responded to her mystical pencil drawing. "It is as if your ego gives a message, that is, your soul gives a reading message. Because the subject of your drawing, which is you in metaphor, has an ancient light in its hands.

I could interpret your drawing as if you tiptoe over your city. You need to light up the village because you don't have confidence."

She said, "I think you're right. Very good. Perhaps I need to draw on the confidence that's deep within which I have felt and experienced before and add it into my next drawing somehow."

He said, "I don't know what's on your mind, but I interpose your drawings as if they were more."

She said, "Yes there is more. We all have types of inner conflict or struggles due to our perceptions."

He said, "However, the woman you draw is you and I have to stop and really understand the message that goes beyond your drawing. I would have to examine all your drawings to make a judgment or an origin of your unconscious. We artists speak through our paintings or sculptures."

She said, "I know it's me somehow and I might not realize what the messages are."

He said, "Underneath our paintings or creations there is always drama."

She said, "Or pain."

He said, "Yes darling, we artists are eternally dissatisfied. The stark reality is this: If I could speak your language well, I would express myself differently, but the translator cannot. Don't be afraid to express yourself with me."

She said, "You express yourself very well because you speak the language of the soul."

He said, "I can understand you."

She said, "I have always been interested in art but there was a period of time when I didn't do very much of it. So, the fact that I have been doing it consistently for a while now is good. It's probably therapeutic for me."

He said, "Art is a form of therapy. A way of straying from our routines."

She said, "Or a way of expressing and releasing
what the mind doesn't understand and the soul needs
to say."

He said, "Sometimes we are dissatisfied, and you
know why. Because not everyone understands who
we are. But when our time on this earth is over
people will appreciate our works or poems, etc.
They will talk about our fragments, the bullshit or
the works that we will leave in this world."

Metaphoric Light

He said, "You fascinate me, a synchronicity, a melding. A huge piece of what's been troubling me in this life and the incentive to shed the old skin.

And honestly, more than the physicality of the beautiful woman. Her mind is the starter fluid of my soul. Her name will be on my lips at the end."

MG

Metaphoric Light

Perspectives

He said, "I think you are too touchy."

She said, "Do you? You can call it touchy; you can label it however you want, but it's still my choice how I respond whether you are aware of the reasons or not.

Actions create reactions. We respond to things, to what we feel, see, and hear. Those responses will tell us much about ourselves if we are paying attention. We also might respond to things which aren't what they seem, and we don't know it.

Sometimes people assume something about us or a situation which isn't what it seems to them. We waste a lot of energy reacting to things which are misperceived or misinterpreted."

Perspectives

Something more wholesome, for love to grow,
For truth to blossom, as debauchery's flung low,
Into the fire, with corruption and filth,
As we begin to realize, what we create through free
will.

Perspectives

Many so-called religious minds are highly
programmed, conditioned, and/or brainwashed.
Some people move beyond belief and into knowing,
into the kingdom within, recognizing that God is
within themselves and others. Not something
separate from themselves.

Certain belief systems are very limited and rigid and
keep people stuck in a type of dogmatic box. It
doesn't allow them to move beyond fear-based
beliefs designed to make them conform. Some
religions take things far too literally and strip away
the spiritual metaphor. It's important to become
aware of how ego functions in certain situations.

Perspectives

People might find fault with what you do, write, or
say … yet they continue to read it. Why? Is it so
they can have something to hate and attack to satisfy
their raging egos? If it's so offensive or misleading,
then don't follow it.

God bless us everyone.

Perspectives

He thought true art had been dead and gone for
centuries.

She said, "People can create beauty from mud and
clay. I don't know if it matters what material one
uses, but rather what they put into it."

Perspectives

Some perspectives might not leave room for or
include other perspectives. When things are too rigid
or extreme there might be suffering and no room for
growth or blossoming.

Perspectives

A private account,
From which to prey,
To hide behind,
To manipulate, to sway.

A game station safe,
From which to pounce,
Upon the unsuspecting,
Who may denounce.

Perspectives

A melody in motion,
A magical tune,
A rhapsody seductive,
Too woo and to swoon.

A soulful vibration,
Where hearts dare to speak,
And the powerful flow,
Of emotions that weep.

Perspectives

Underlying Hostility

Underlying hostility,
In the workplace, what a drag,
People waging battles from within,
Looking for a place to plant their flag.

There are battle zones we witness,
Where only one person participates,
But they might pull in more recruitments,
To their paradigm of hate.

Battlefields reflecting,
What's within, the aggressor can't see,
Feeling justified to judge and attack,
From an energy unfree.

Sometimes we're just an observer,
And we must be careful not to get drawn in,
To what people who might be two-faced,
Don't recognize as sin.

To sin which means to miss the point,
To sin which means to miss the mark,
Not in alignment with their own truth and love,
And dim the inner spark.

Janine Palmer (Silver Moon)

About the Author

Janine Palmer (Silver Moon) is a writer of esoteric and energy healing messages. She writes from her own healing experiences and observations which lead to deeper wisdom.

She is a Clinical Hypnotherapist and Shamanic Practitioner who is passionate about emotional and spiritual healing.

She speaks of sacred truth, hidden keys, and light and shadow. She reminds us to remember, honor and embrace our divine worthiness and to step out of programming.

She shines light on the power of forgiveness and the beauty we hold within. Her work might be helpful or of interest to those working through the initiations of spiritual alchemy and realigning to the love we always are, our innate truth.

~ I think people feel your kind energy – WB

~ Right words – AF

~ **Great words and works – SW**

~ I don't think I ever read this one my friend. Kind of hits a dark spot for my memory bank. Oh, so true in the passage. Vent I shall do, enlighten my darkest tent. Thanks, my sage – JM

~ True – AL

~ Reminds me of someone….? – SW

~ As excellent as ever my friend – JM

~ You write as my life unfolds. I love this work of yours – SD

~ Prizewinner – SW

~ **Simply beautiful gift of words – SD**

~ Always love your poetic tales – JM

~ The Spirit Eternal – SW

~ That is awesome Janine! – TAM

~ So beautiful, so much truth weaving through the rhymes… - AA

~ You have good energy – WB

~ Beautiful!!! – CH

~ Really beautiful words and a way forward for us all – SD

~ Love this! – AS

~ **The timely truth well spoken – BS**

~ Thank you Beautiful! – AS

~ Healing purpose. Every touch has left its mark – AL

~ Very well said!! One person's illusion is not mandatory for all to participate in – BS

~ Love this! It's Beautiful – AS

~ Perfect – DSC

~ True – MB

~ **You have a really chill vibe. Love it and I think people feel your kind energy – WB**

~ Definitely like this piece Janine – SD

~ Another beautiful piece you created – DB

~ I love this warrior! – UL

~ So true, so true – GM

~ Beautiful – GH

~ **Your talent should be rewarded because what you write you do with grace very naturally. Because you are able to transport any person to imagine living in these stories with natural familiarity – AF**

~ Absolutely loved this – SD

~ **Persevere in what you write. Never give up because you have a gift to transport anyone who reads. Run, find a publisher because there is so much to read in your stories and poems – AF**

~ Beautifully written my friend – JM

~ Beautiful, this little verse, because there is a lot of imagination, "The clip clop of hooves over the forest path." Congratulations because you have an innate talent – AF

~ **Keep writing because one day you will be
rewarded because what you write strikes like
lightning inside the hearts of those who love art –
AF**

~ Must say Janine, not only liked the subject and the
way I got drawn in for a moment or two, but it took
into a different realm which I took on board and liked,
to be honest – SD

~ For clarity, see your mirror – SW

~ Love this! – CH

~ Look in mirror to see a giver – SW

~ Janine, you have an exceptional talent – AF

~ Compassion – SW

~ **As you write the stories, I just close my eyes and
imagine the story you wrote. Exciting because you
have an imagination that can transport anyone
who reads – AF**

~ Love – TMM

~ Sweet – MCM

~ Great words – DB

~ I like it, like the theme and the way you expressed
it – MG

~ Awesome!! – UL

~ Excellent post full of truth – DS

~ Speaks volumes – MG

~ **This poem is awesome. To tell it like it is in such
a poetic way. You are so gifted with words. Thank
you. I shared it. I love your drawings – MCM**

~ Wow!! This is amazing!! So real and profound –
GE

~ Well done beautiful soul – WGB

~ **Just wow for now. Have a lot to absorb with this
one. Excellent job my profound author – JM**

~ Very emotive – JC

~ Very good – DS

~ So perfect in every way sister – TMM

~ Nice – SS

~ **I'm happy your poems still pop up in the
memories section. I hope that your posts start
showing up on my feed now. I've loved your words
since I first saw them several years ago – PW**

~ Love this! – MM

~ **I love and appreciate you so much. I'm one of
your Biggest Fans – TSP**

~ Truth Janine – JA

~ Thank you – DR

~ I love the darkest poems because they are actually
the ones that make you realize the value of life
because basically life is full of existential problems. I
don't love poems with happy endings – AF

~ Love this, Janine Palmer! – DS

~ What was, what will be and what is…God – BW

~ That it is – GL

~ Stunning – SD

~ Wow! Amazing! – SL

~ **Thank you. Beautiful energy – CS**

~ Beautiful – JM

~ **Your writing is perfect for what is going on in this world – MCM**

~ You're prolific and they make sense to me – MG

~ Excellent write! – KMT

~ Sharing – AS

~ True – KG

~ **EXQUISITE – RF**

~ For Sure – SW

~ **There is a lot in there – MK**

~ Full of true love – JM

~ This just resonates – MG

~ POWERFUL LOVE – RF

~ **Beautifully penned my friend – JM**

~ **So many thoughts here to think of... – JS**

~ Favourite – AS

~ With your writings you might get through to the one who needs it. I remember that feeling I had when I'd first read what you'd written. It rang so true to me that it opened my eyes and I think back to 6 – 7 years ago, I was a mess. And I contribute a lot of my recovery to you. If you plant that mustard seed, 100 people might be unaffected, but that one is – MG

~ BEATUFIUL NATURE OF LIFE – RF

~ Wow this is grabbing me. You're really nailing this. This is beautiful, I'm saving this. I keep reading it over and over and I catch things in it. I love this. You just shine – MG

~ Very well said – AS

~ Amen – JM

~ You see and feel a lot with the higher divinity. You're very intelligent and very in tune with the realms that some people cannot see or feel. I love reading your stuff. I've actually been reading a lot of it lately. You're absolutely brilliant. Keep it going – WB

~ Analyzing your good work – MG

~ Reflection brings us changes. Different ways of seeing things – AF

~ **I love what you do. Your writing is very healing - WB**

~ Reminds me of Psalms 12:6-7 which seems timely – SW

~ Amen – RR

~ Yes – SW

~ "Judge not, lest ye be judged – Blessed are they which are persecuted for righteousness' sake; for theirs is the kingdom of heaven." Mathew Chapter 5 in its entirety – SW

~ Janine is spot on in regard to translation(s) through the millennia – SW

~ Loved everything written here and holding onto my own thoughts and dreams of who I am, and my journey and beliefs to get me here – SD

~ You just have that beautiful, spiritual feeling. You are an abundant of healing energy and knowledge – WB

~ I felt white light around you the first time I interacted with you on social media – DE

~ Beautifully said – KH

~ I need that. Thanks – ML

~ Many languages on many levels and many dimensions – BS

~ Well stated – JM

~ People fear your wisdom, 'honestly, truth – because you are a messenger from the highest order and people fear your light. The light of humanity that wipes away the darkness and shows us our divine presence and glory to serve but one true God. And serve it you must – SD

~ Love this! – CH

~ I stand with Janine's writings – JA

~ Too many questions you are asking yourself, too many issues to evaluate in an uncertain world. We all ask questions or say our thoughts about everything, but why despair to seek answers in a world that does not belong to us? – AF

~ Janine Palmer, true your light touches many – AKK

~ Your advice is strong and correct – TM

~ Love this one. Peace to you – JM

~ Incredible! – MB

~ Nice post. Thanks for taking the time to write it –
MK

~ Amen! God is Love! No judgment! – MB

~ Love this beautiful Sister poet!!! – CH

~ Finding it is the journey – BS

~ Religion is a deadly subject. Too many different
cultures. Obviously, people will never understand
that there is only one God…maybe in your culture he
will be called Jehovah...or with another name, but the
fact remains that God is one called in different ways
and there is no war in the name of God, there is no
holy war you could wage in the name of God – AF

~ **Spot On! – DD**

~ Amen – KCS

~ Seem to be walking simultaneously along a similar
path – JM

~ Perhaps My Favorite – SW

~ Love this beautiful Sister poet!!! – CH

~ **Intrigued – MB**

~ This – LLW

~ Eloquently phrased – TMM

~ Smiles for miles – RD

~ **Well written words with soulful knowledge, as is
your usual – GL**

~ Totally get this – SD

~ @UR4 realization with words – GL

~ Wow – MB

~ Yes and yes connected – GL

~ Represent – RFG

~ I really like this – NP

~ Perfectly said! – MCM

~ Thank you for sharing – DB

~ **Thanks for helping us see the light – JM**

~ Love the words – SD

~ You're such a blessing to everyone around you! – MW

~ **Truth. Beautiful words – MCM**

~ Excellence – MS

~ Just beautiful – SD

~ So beautiful – CH

~ **Uplifting – SW**

~ Your words on paper are beautiful – DB

~ Fantastic Ink Beautiful! – CH

~ Very Good!! – MK

~ You should read your poems more often. They make it a higher value – AF

~ Reminds me of a strong woman with a dragon as her guardian – SD

~ **Love seeing the Truth – AS**

~ I like that. That's catchy. It's good stuff Janine, it really is – MG

~ Yes, yes, yes! Beautiful! – AS

~ Connecting @4real, natural, liking your word power – GL

~ Beautifully written – MCM

~ Absolutely gorgeous – NFW

~ So wonderful – TM

~ Just Amazing Ink beautiful! – CH

~ **Divinely worded – SW**

~ Your poetry is right for anyone to read – AF

~ This is also a delight – TM

~ I see you have embraced the spiritual and that is beautiful – KU

~ Thank you, Janine – DR

~ **Wow, another dandy. You have a unique way of expressing your awareness of the mystery of being human and the power of love. Your words are eloquently graceful and moving – MG**

~ You have a caring heart and your compassion is undeniable – KU

~ Just magic filled. Thank you – TMM

~ Great post my friend – JM

~ Lovely – DR

~ POETIC JUSTICE!!! THANK YOU, Janine Palmer – SL

~ Janine Palmer you really have a holy way of expression – TMM

~ **Absolutely beautiful. I love your imagery and the hope you offer, in the dark. You have such a gift with words. I truly appreciate that you see a way to get to the light at the end of the tunnel. It's hard to do sometimes – MW**

www.ingramcontent.com/pod-product-compliance
Lightning Source LLC
Chambersburg PA
CBHW061339160726
47995CB00001B/100